BEYOND BABYSITTING

DEEPENING YOUR KIDS CHURCH JOURNEY

ANNE SILLARS

Ark House Press
arkhousepress.com

Unless otherwise stated, all Scriptures are taken from the New International Translation (Holy Bible. Copyright© 1996, 2004, 2007, 2013 by Tyndale House Foundation. Used by permission of Tyndale House Publishers Inc., Carol Stream, Illinois 60188. All rights reserved.)

Cataloguing in Publication Data:
Title: Beyond Babysitting
ISBN: 978-1-7642813-2-4 (pbk)
Subjects: REL109020 RELIGION / Christian Ministry / Children; REL109030 RELIGION / Christian Ministry / Youth; REL091000 RELIGION / Christian Education / Children & Youth.

Design by initiateagency.com

TABLE OF CONTENTS

ACKNOWLEDGEMENTS

To those who've walked with me and helped read and edit, thank you for encouraging me to write this book when I was unsure.

To all who've been part of our kids' teams over years, your faithful hearts, love for Jesus and desire to see His children being fully activated have been God's gift to Paul & my hearts - thank you.

To our Pastors over the years who've entrusted us with such a precious part of church, enabling & resourcing us to such incredible levels - thank you for the highest privilege in the Kingdom of God.

To my children, Toby & Kai who've enabled Mum & Dad to serve God in this way by being up early on Sunday mornings, helping prep so many elements, for doing what needed to be done and letting us be on your "turf". We know God has His hand powerfully on you both.

To my husband, Paul - the biggest kid out, who loves God with the simplicity of a child! You have been sanity on the insane days. You always dare to believe for bigger things from our very, very, very, big God!

To God, who has taken our offering of five squishy loaves, and two stinky fish and fed many over the years. Will You take this offering and again make it more than enough for those who need it.

To those who hold this book, you do so because God has placed something precious in your heart to see something more. May you hear His voice guiding, His heart beating, and may He open your eyes to how He sees the children in your church. You may not feel like you are enough to do this, but He is more than enough.

INTRODUCTION

Whether you have been involved in kids work for years, or whether you have just started in kids work, this book is for you. It's an intensely down to earth handbook of how to do all the practical elements of kids work, whilst at the same time taking what you do from "safe babysitting" to ministering in a way that is fully fired up. The goal is to produce world changing, active church members, just perhaps in smaller packages!

For years I have been captivated by God's perspective on children. When we look at the Bible, in Matthew 18:1-6 we discover how Jesus saw children. The context here is that His disciples are having a conversation, or perhaps an argument, about which one of them is the greatest in the Kingdom of Heaven. Jesus contrasts their self-centred pride by calling a child to Him and elevates the child! How? Well, for one, it indicates there were children around listening to Jesus – interesting given He'd just finished some fairly heavy teaching on divorce! Apparently, He was OK with that, more than OK, it would seem. So, Jesus brings the child into the centre of the group. Then in verse 3, He shockingly goes even further by saying that unless the adults (including the highly educated adults) became like children they would never enter the Kingdom of Heaven. What quality in the child, or indeed children, meant they could easily enter the Kingdom of Heaven?

In Verse 4, it tells us that their humility is what will cause them to be the greatest – and they weren't even trying to be the greatest!

Verse 5 tells us that receiving a child in Jesus' name is the very same as receiving Jesus Himself. Why is that the requirement? Let's get real. In our adult heads we think way too much – and primarily about ourselves, if we are honest. However, when we follow the example of a child, we very quickly realise that they are wired far more simply than we, and that's the way we are meant to be wired. We're not meant to be complicated. We're meant to come to Jesus simply, humbly, with trust, eagerly, excitedly and without mental gymnastics (and maybe with a few physical gymnastics instead).

Let me ask you when was the last time that you were so excited to come into Jesus' presence that you jumped or cartwheeled in?

There's another occasion that we see that Jesus elevated children as an example to adults. When His own disciples tried to stop children from coming into His presence (Matt 19:14) He brought correction to the adults, not to the children. This bible scene can often elicit pictures of Jesus sitting surrounded by nicely behaved children, all sitting on the ground around Him. Wherever in the Bible did it say THAT happened? Is that truly how Jesus would have related to them? Our views of children, including how we tend to view children in church, can seem to stem from the way children were seen and treated in the Victorian era. Somehow, we believe that "well behaved" children are quiet children, and that children should be seen and not heard… but there is nothing Biblical about that! We are richer when we change our mindset about how Jesus sees children and reject the Victorian perspective.

Becoming like children can help us start to accept children's places in our churches and enable us to make ways for them to encounter Jesus. I have learnt so much about faith from children. With children, when God has said something in His word, they simply believe it, they are expectant that their God will hear and answer. I have found that if I want to press into God for breakthrough, children will easily come into that place. We follow

Jesus' teaching and example when we follow a child's example. Watch them, learn from them about how to understand the Bible and engage with what God has said. They explore curiously and they work in visuals which helps me as an adult gain greater revelation. Children are incredibly creative, another major element of God's nature – they aren't limited in vision, they have the biggest imaginations and they are easily Holy Spirit led. By watching a child, you will learn about how to enter His presence easily and with joy as they trust and easily engage with Him. Hear me right – I am not anti-adult! This perspective is Biblical. When Jesus pulled a child out and put them right in the middle of a load of adults, He was saying look how they do it, and don't you dare make them complicate faith like you do (He's very clear on that in verse 6).

Let's take a look at the numbers. What is the percentage of under 18s in your church? What is the percentage of under 12s? Are we disregarding a large proportion of our church because we decided they were too young to count? Our churches are richer places when the equality of the kingdom of God extends to the percentage of church that are children.

Have you ever heard people say that kids are the church of tomorrow? When someone says this to me, they tend to receive an impassioned response of "NO! They're the church with us today!"

INTRODUCTION

The concept that kids don't step into being part of church until they're 18 is simply not true, we've already seen it's not Biblical, and when we stop and think about it, this thinking degrades kids church to the level of babysitting. Sadly, our children in church have been relegated to a cultural place that is somehow lesser than adults. We as adults act as though we are always the teachers, and children are always the students, but it's just not true and Jesus didn't think so either.

If you long for more in your church, that is what this book is about! Encouraging, building up, enabling, and empowering our children to be an equally valued part of church - Spirit filled, on fire for Jesus! Activated and functioning within our churches. If you want to see revival, if you want to see miracles, if you want to hear the voice of God, perhaps adjust your viewpoint. A child in your church may well be the one that God has placed to lead the way, the one that He appointed to pray with you, or have a word for you. Wouldn't it be incredible if all age groups in our church were fully on fire for Jesus? Surely at that point we would see revival!

This book is divided into two sections: Part 1 - The Heart and Part 2 - The Practicalities. Please resist jumping straight to the second section. Implementing practical steps without understanding the heart will only have limited success. This book is also written in the first person. My husband Paul and I have had the privilege of being a part of leading kids church, and kids' missions for over 50 years between the two of us. My desire is that this would be easy to read, just as if I was talking to you in person. I love to tell story, so hopefully this way of writing will be straightforward and help you truly get a hold of what God wants to say.

THE HEART

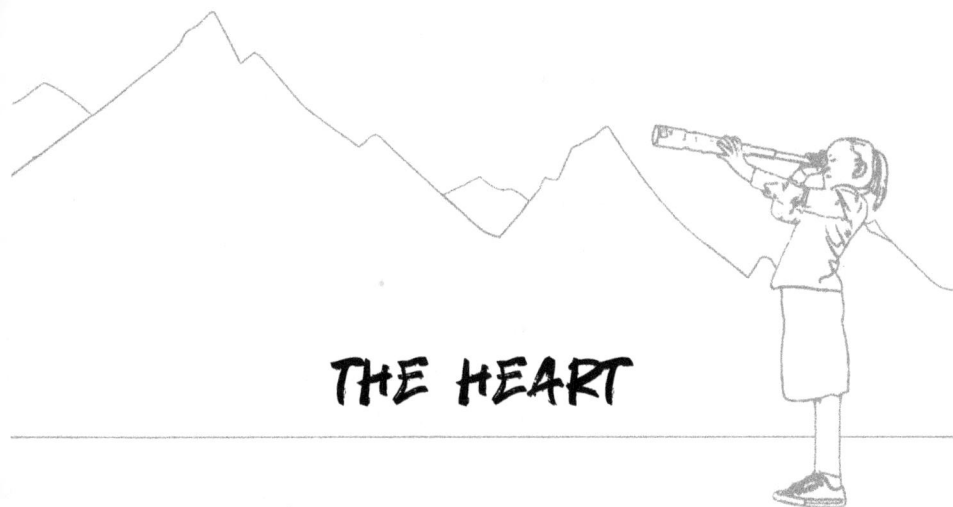

Let's look a little closer at what God has in His heart for our children and His church.

The Hungry Generation

As I mentioned, my husband and I have been involved in kids work and kids church a long time, since 1990. Over our years in ministry, we have begun to see a new young generation that is crazy hungry for God. If we look at our world context, it seems that the world has in many ways become much darker, and there really is very little hope for this generation outside of Jesus. Economically, health-wise, socially - the outlook is bleak. Perhaps there is the same amount of darkness, but for this generation it is reinforced regularly in the media, on the internet and through conversations, where they are reminded on a daily basis about wars, suicide, anxiety, pain, and crisis. Unless the church steps in, there is no one telling them that there is hope, light and life.

Often in kids church the emphasis has been upon having fun. Even in my generation, kids church was about having a lot of fun. However, this new generation is continually entertained. "Fun" is on demand at the push of a button, but they're bored of it. They long for meaning. I am not saying kids church should be a lecture or boring, but we're not there to entertain them, any more than we're there to babysit them. We are there to draw them into the presence of God - into an encounter with Him. There needs to be God's life bursting right through it. We have seen large groups of kids become still for prolonged periods of time as we've simply prayed for the Holy Spirit to fill them up. We have seen them just rested in His presence so much so that the adults don't know what to do. We have seen kids lead others (including adults) in church to receive a miracle because they are so sensitive to the moving of the Spirit of God. They love God's presence, they want to hear His voice, they want to hear Him speak to them about their calling. They are the Hungry Generation. Totally - be fun, but whatever you do, do not become entertainment. Lead them, minister to them, petition God for them and enable them to touch heaven.

Kids believe quickly

I remember when my own son was barely two years old, speaking to him about how God wants to talk to him personally. I saw him light up at this truth - that God would talk to HIM! I explained that it might be through a picture, a word, or a dream. Straight away he was up for it. "Well, what does God want to say?" he asked. Caught a bit off guard at his eagerness to hear God right in that moment, I suggested we pray that God would show him something and speak to him in a way he would understand. Within moments he said "Mum! I've got it, I see a drum" rather surprised I asked him what kind of drum it was – a ratta tatta kind of drum, or a boomdy boomdy drum. "No Mum" was his rather frustrated reply, "an eardrum." In our church service that Sunday, he shared that picture and three people were healed! You see, even at a young age kids see and hear from God, and fast! This is likely because they actually believe that God will speak. Their natural level of expectation and imagination when connected with the Holy Spirit becomes a powerhouse to release signs and words from Heaven.

I remember having a mum call me about her child who was only four years old at the time. We had been learning a memory verse in Philippians 4:6 about praying instead of worrying. It became apparent to the child that at home the mum had been worrying about something or talking about being worried. Her child was like "mum why are you worrying when the Bible says…" – and quoted the verse word for word. She was highly challenged in that moment of worry and totally blown away that her child had ministered to her so powerfully! How did it happen? The Word of God was spoken out and had taken root in her child and the child believed that the truth of Scripture would change her mum's behaviour!

Kids trust

Connection to the Holy Spirit and the Word of God produces incredible faith to believe for things and creates a sense of expectation. As adults, we place a high value on understanding and on knowledge. Yet faith doesn't have an intellectual requirement. It isn't about what you know, or what you have worked out, but who you know. Faith is about reaching out to someone we trust. When we trust that God loves us, and that He's good, we simply put our hand in His. Kids can do that! And they do it really well - often way better than we adults. The Bible is full of the language of God being our Father. Jesus talks about God as our Father in Matthew 7:11: "If you, then, though you are evil, know how to give good gifts to your children, how much more will your Father in Heaven give good gifts to those who ask him!"

God says treat me like I'm your Father. Come to me because I am your Father. Come into My presence unafraid, unashamed, trusting, and knowing that I am good. Kids will believe for the biggest of miracles because they trust the One whose hand they hold. Do we? Or do we get brought down by our adult overthinking? Children lead us and show us that we don't need to understand or have great knowledge to believe. It's not an intellectual exercise; we just need to reach out our hand.

If you follow this truth, you'll understand why I want to just spend a moment now talking about babies. Because surely it is babysitting when it comes to babies. They don't understand anything you're saying, right? Wrong! Babies know the presence of God perhaps more than at any other age. Once again, we need to challenge ourselves as to why we have made faith an intellectual thing. The best things we can do in a nursery setting with a load of babies is pray, praise and worship, and read the Word of God. I have seen babies respond animatedly when the presence of God has come upon them. They know the One who formed and fashioned them in the womb. As we pray over them, declaration goes forth, the words of our lips hit their hearts and whilst they might not say Amen (that would be a surprise!), truth is established within them and over them. When we praise God, the joy that is in us is coupled with their non-verbal joy. In that moment high praise is lifted to Heaven. When we worship with a baby, Heaven comes down and they are learning, experiencing and responding to His presence. When we speak the Word of God with them, we establish in their hearts and minds a love for His truth. Yes of course we look after their physical needs. They are babies after all, and it is vital that we care for them practically to the highest level. BUT this isn't daycare - it's kids church and in kids church we have the privilege to be able to pray, praise, worship and speak God's word to them and over them.

Surely a baby is the best example of one who trusts the hands that hold them? They know God's peace and rest, they know what it is to have done absolutely nothing to deserve love and care, and yet they receive it. They truly understand and accept love. In Luke 1:44, we hear of a baby who is not yet born leaping for joy at the recognition of their Messiah, which brings forth a prophecy from the lips of Elizabeth. Don't tell me babies don't know their God! Again, faith is about trust, and kids, especially babies, are an incredible example of that.

More than a verbal expression

So, we know that faith isn't an intellectual exercise. Let me push it a step further and suggest that verbal communication skills are therefore not required for a relationship with God. How do children communicate? On the whole with young children their communication is typically less verbal and more about movements and senses. That's why they love running, jumping, hugs, tickles, and being showered with hundreds of kisses. God knows that, He made them that way! He made them wired for movement. So again, why do we make their faith something that has to be expressed using words whilst being still? Sitting still is not the best way to pray with most 3-year-olds, in fact it is not the best way to do anything with a 3-year-old! If you don't believe me, you should try it!

Why can't we pray whilst hopping on one leg or whilst wiggling our fingers? Do we feel that this is in some way disrespectful to God? However, God is our Father and we are invited at the very least to come to Him the way we would come to our earthly dad. When they were younger, my son and daughter would come to us hopping, jumping, twirling, cartwheeling. Why would we be upset by that as parents? Why then, would we think God would be upset by it? They are made to move and it's a part of their heart expression towards Him and their means of communicating with Him. How is that a lesser expression of faith?

In fact, if we look in Revelation and the picture of worship in Heaven, we get a way bigger picture of the relationship between worship and movement! Read Revelation chapters 4 and 5 and you will see stones that sparkle, flashes of lightning, roars of thunder, torches burning, a glass sea sparkling, four living creatures singing (possibly whilst flying), twenty-four elders kneeling, casting down their crowns before the throne, scrolls being opened, millions of angels singing and then the elders falling down before the throne in worship. I don't know about you, but that sounds to me like a lot of movement! I think it would also be quite loud. Heaven and the worship in Heaven is wild and sensory. This is perfect for children. Can you imagine their eyes light up at this kind of praise and worship?

Let me therefore ask a question. If we want to give our kids the opportunity to enter God's presence before the age of seven or eight years old, why would we give them songs with subtitled words when they can't even read? It doesn't even make logical sense! Surely, it's better to give them songs with simple movements/dances they can follow. If we want to engage them in prayer – talking with God - how about having pictures that enable them to choose what they want to pray for? They can then hold those pictures and touch, cuddle or kiss them, even as we adults provide the verbal articulation that they can copy. Or let's zoom around the room and shout our prayers as we fly to get close to God? If we want to read the Word of God, why can't we read it separately and then chat about it over morning tea? Often, Jesus talked about serious stuff whilst eating with his disciples. Just look at the Last Supper, one of the most serious and important moments in the Gospels. He chooses to talk to the disciples over dinner. Did He know that His disciples would pay the most attention whilst eating? God meets us where we are, and it's the same for our kids. Why can't we act out the stories? He doesn't need them to respond to Him as an adult would. He's not waiting for them to grow up so He can encounter them. He delights in their childlike response, right now.

Physical expressions of our faith

God also made us physical beings, He could have made us "mind beings" or "soul beings", but He didn't. Therefore, our worship and connection with Him needs to involve our physicality. In a time of praising Him, have you ever felt you can't jump high enough to express your gratitude to Him? In a time of worship are you unable to express what's in your heart until you kneel or prostrate yourself? He gave us tithing as a physical expression of the giving of our heart. He gave us the altar as a place to sacrifice our lives before Him. He gave us communion to help us have a physical stimulus to remember, and to partake of Him. Again, these are all physical expressions, that for children they will easily and beautifully grasp to connect with Him. So, the more physical expressions of worship that we can include in kids church the better.

Let us also remember that our God is a creative God, and He gives us creativity. Let's use that creativity that is God-given to not only help our kids to engage with Him in physical ways, but also to help the adults on team do so. In the setting of kids church, we have found that the team have engaged with Him on a deeper level in this physicality. We have touched Heaven in powerful ways as we've developed our communication to God to be more than words. We have even had team members who prefer the freedom and depth of praise and worship in kids church compared to main church!

Godly imaginations and the Word of God

Our kids might not get excited by exegesis or systematic theology, but kids LOVE the Word of God. Their ability to imagine is far better and more regularly used than ours. Imagination is a God-given gift that we tend to leave behind as we grow, but from our imaginations come creativity, solutions, ideas, miracles and understanding. When we approach the Word of God as adults, we often just read the words. In contrast, kids tend to engage easily with it. The Bible is full of incredible miracles, images, dreams, animals, and adventures! What is not to love about it? If they are hiding in a tent because they are being "Jonah in the belly of the whale" it will be difficult not to become totally immersed as an adult and gain insights from them as they explore what Jonah went through. We once spent a session talking about the Israelites crossing the Red Sea with water piled up on other side and the Egyptian army chasing them. I was floored when one child asked, "Do you think they could see the fish?" My slightly confused answer was followed by a list of questions that included:

- Would there have been crocodiles?
- What about octopus?
- Would they be stuck half-way out of the water?
- Could the Israelites pull them out?

I don't know about you, but I'd never stopped to consider these practicalities and the impact of this on the Israelites as they were chased across the Red Sea. I'd thought about the ground that they walked on because Scripture talks about it. However, I'd never thought to examine the wonder of those two pillars of water and the kinds of practical details that came with it. I came away and re-examined the passage in a totally new way as God gave me fresh revelation of how He brings us into freedom.

Vision building with kids

I've already talked about how easily kids grasp God's perspective. One of the most powerful things that can be done as a church is to involve kids church with any vision cast. Whether that's a building project, a new direction, or a new service, kids will bring enthusiasm, vision and insight. Paul and I had an incredible time with one group of kids who were part of a church that was located on a large but undeveloped factory site. We did a whole vision session with cardboard boxes, tubes and all kinds of craft materials as we allowed the kids to build what they saw God had for the church going forward. There was of course a lolly shop somewhere on the site, but their understanding of God's bigger perspective for the site and the role it would play in the surrounding community both encouraged and challenged the leadership when we presented it to them. I'm not suggesting you give the kids the architectural plans to draw up, but they are more than able to catch and understand a vision! More than that, as a valued part of the church they could be given opportunities to both catch the vision of the church and extend it in a way that only a child can.

Raising our expectations

I hope this section about the heart behind kids church has been helpful. Our children have the very life, breath and Spirit of God in them. To reference Jennifer Toledo in her incredible book "Children and the Supernatural", they don't get some watered down, half power Holy Spirit. When they get filled with the Holy Spirit they get filled with the whole power that raised Jesus Christ from the dead! Raise your expectations, change your thinking, because these kids have been gifted into your care by God Himself. In doing so, He charges you with great responsibility. Dare to believe that He has more for them than you've ever imagined, not just in the future but right now. Children are as much His chosen ministers of His Good News as any adult. Remember that these children long for His presence and will respond to His touch and His love so very quickly.

Give them opportunities and space to have a voice, to experience, to serve, to share, to hear, to pray, to praise and to worship the One who wired us all this way. They are a huge part of the church, and we exclude them to our detriment. Don't limit what God wants to do in them and through them. If you feel ill-equipped for the task ahead, remember "He who calls you is faithful; He will surely do it". (1 Thess 5:25)

THE PRACTICALITIES

Ok so now you've got the heart of kids church and you want to make things happen. This next section will hopefully help you with the "how."

A part of the church

You may now be all stirred up to do things differently. However, before you go rushing off, please go and talk with your pastors. Tell them what God has laid on your heart to do. Make sure you have their permission to go further. They may think you're a little crazy but that's OK, enthusiasm often looks crazy! Many pastors haven't spent a sustained time in the land of kids church, it's just something they're grateful for and often just "magically happens." However, if God has laid something on your heart, you need to share it with them, because they are the ones anointed and appointed to lead the church of which you are a part.

If you don't get the permission you need, do not think that your pastors are mean or bad. It might not be the decision you would make, but getting hurt, frustrated or offended will not help. Bear in mind this has come to you as a Godly revelation. It is God's church, and He is more than able to reveal more to your pastors if this is the right time to do so. Even if He doesn't - will you continue to obey and trust Him that He knows what He's doing? Make sure you keep your relationship with your pastors strong and sweet. You never know how God will bring forth a perfect time further down the track when you can speak again. Like a child, put your hand in His and trust Him.

If you do get permission, then make sure to regularly check back with your pastors and keep them updated on what is changing. If miracles start happening in kids church, no one will know if you don't communicate with your pastor! Telling everyone else before you've told the pastor will not go well either! Once again, they have a God given responsibility to lead the church, and we need to make sure that we support and enable this, particularly in the way we communicate about an area that is often unseen. If your pastor gives you the opportunity to share about kids church in the main church don't duck it, SHARE! Wouldn't it be incredible if the sharing of a move of the Holy Spirit in kids church sparked a fresh move of the Holy Spirit amongst the adults? When we are released in this way we can promote and advocate for the kids within the church. In that place you will have a unique opportunity to tell everyone what God is doing in the hearts of the kids.

Don't forget the power of testimony. When you have kids who are being impacted, perhaps there's the opportunity (with the right parental permission and media release forms) for you to film the child telling what God's done. It doesn't need to be long, in fact short is often better. Sometimes if a child is unsure, a little interview is a great way to go – why don't you or their parent sit with them and just chat (whilst recording it) as to what God did. Don't make it a scary thing. At the very least you can show the testimony to your pastors, which will both encourage them personally and help link them in more with what God has for kids church.

How to bring in change well.

Before I address any of the elements in this section, let's address this first point very, very clearly.

DO NOT CHANGE EVERYTHING AT ONCE!!!

"No one likes change, unless it's change that they've implemented" (Randall Lee). I heard this preached a number of years ago and I've remembered it all these years. It's so very true. We all think we're up for change until it's somebody else's change that is brought upon us.

I remember coming into the role of Kids Pastor at a church which was much bigger than previous churches in which we'd been involved. That year I went to a national conference, where God gave me significant encouragement. I was talking with one of the speakers after a session and explained that I'd just taken this role on but was daunted because there was so much to change. Their response was "but at least you know where you're going"! They then prayed with me and their word was "God says you have everything you need". Encouraged by that I went back to God and asked for a strategy to implement all the change that I knew needed to happen. He gave me a very simple answer - change one thing at a time and sustain it. Not surprisingly the heavenly strategy worked! Why do we still get surprised by that!

That strategy, combined with a lot of communication with our team, enabled us to navigate a huge season of change. Instead of overwhelming our precious team with a lot of changes all at once, changing one thing at a time and sustaining it meant that the team and the kids were able to handle the changes and come out strong.

Fix small things up

As you change things, and even as you continue week in week out, one of the best things we did was bring in feedback forms. Now the reason for these was because we were running 4 different rooms at 3 services. There was no way that we could meet with all the teams after every service. So, there was a feedback form in every room, in every resource box, for every service. Having expressed to the team that I wanted these filled in every time, initially they felt that it was just another thing to do. However, over time they came to realise that this gave me the opportunity to know very quickly about issues, both big and small. The feedback forms meant that as we brought in changes, immediately they could communicate to me what worked and what didn't work and why, even if I was not there in person. In turn, this meant that the plan for the following week could be tweaked to accommodate their feedback.

One example of this was when we had moved one age group to a different room. The team that first week discovered that a particular game that the kids loved to play did not work in the new room, because it had carpet as flooring. They put it on the feedback form that week and we could immediately ensure that we did not schedule that game when we used that room. Another time was when we were doing water play in the toddlers room and the team were able to communicate on the form not just the issue that the floor became slippery, but also their suggestion to fix the issue. By the following week the simple fix was implemented and the team were delighted. My team knew I was listening to them, and so their sense of value increased, which in turn increased their commitment to the team.

The form included simple sections, such as listing resources that were running low and any issues with the building (for example: a ceiling tile was wet and bulging or that the fencing was working loose). It also included sections where the team could tell me about a craft that didn't work and why, or the impact of a prayer strategy with the kids. On every level, they knew that I wanted to know, and I wanted to support them and make it easier for them.

All of these elements give you a much higher rate of success as a leader, because you're not just relying on what you notice but you now have many other sets of eyes all also noticing and caring and bringing about change.

However, prepare your heart folks, because the flip side to this is that sometimes the feedback can feel very personal. When you've poured your heart into an element of programming and then the words on the feedback form simply say "it didn't work" or even worse "it didn't work and I knew it wouldn't!" you do have to take it on. If you ask for feedback, know that sometimes there will be those moments when you have to take a deep breath and choose not to take it as a personal attack. Generally, it is not truly a personal attack anyway. As you build relationships with your team members, you'll learn their way of speaking, and that will help in some of these moments.

So, what do you do when you get that kind of feedback? If they simply write that it didn't work, go back to them and say "hey tell me more, what happened, let's get this right together so it works for the next team".

If they add the second swipe to your heart, go back to them, but perhaps this time ask "hey are you ok you sound frustrated?" They might be frustrated with something totally unrelated to kids church, but that moment in kids church was the last straw. You can totally talk with them and pray into that with them. They might be frustrated with kids church. Make sure you also don't take that personally. If they are frustrated, then hear them out, let them be honest, and then just prayerfully walk with them if you can. If you can't, then get someone from the adult leadership team to walk with them. If you've hurt them, apologise and ask for their grace. We are called first and foremost to love God and love each other, and by this will all those watching in the world know that we are His (John 13:35). If you need help navigating that, go to your pastor/oversight and get help. This does not mean you are the wrong person for the role, nor does it mean God has not called you to do this. Your battle is not with the person on your team who's told you this stuff. The Bible tells us clearly that our battle is NOT with flesh and blood, but against rulers and principalities (Eph 6:12) of which your precious team member is neither. I can tell you this, if you are starting to press into believing for more from God in kids church you are going to start to be on the receiving end of a few battles. There are a number of rulers and principalities who would much rather you went back to babysitting!

THE PRACTICALITIES

FOUNDATIONS

Pray, pray and keep praying

"Yes of course," you say. "I know this bit." Ok, well let's just make sure we agree. Psalm 127 (ESV) makes it very clear – "Unless the Lord builds the house, those who build it labour in vain. Unless the Lord watches over the city, the watchman stays awake in vain." Fruitful kids church is not about picking a successful pattern or programme. Nor is it about having the best infrastructure. Programmes will not change kids' lives, God will. It's His house, they're His kids, and we work with the precious team He's given to us. It's pretty dramatic to say unless the Lord builds, we work in vain. There's a part of me that would want to say, "But God, we did some good right?" Scripture is clear, our work is meaningless, useless, without point UNLESS He is the builder. Let's be clear again: Jesus very clearly says He builds the church. We have our part to play, and we work hard. Some days in kids church we work very hard. Yet it is He who builds, He who anoints and He who transforms.

So pray! Pray for the kids in your church, allow God to show you them as He sees them, let Him break your heart for them. Pray for your team, protection over them, for the Holy Spirit to fill them, for unity between you. Pray for your kids' families. Pray for the leadership who care for them.

Once you've prayed for that, pray practically with your team. Pray for vision, for strategies and for clarity. Pray for creativity in your programmes, for problem solving abilities, for provision and resources, for more team members, for joy and peace in the rooms and for the Holy Spirit to rest on each room. If God has called you, He also wants to equip you and He does that when we ask Him.

It's not school

Once they're four or five, our kids go to school five days a week, forty weeks a year. Depending on the child, they will have varying attitudes towards school and learning. Whilst some techniques of teaching and school programmes can be useful, kids church is not putting God in a box alongside their learning about mathematics and history. That is a "learning about", whereas in kids church we aim for an "encounter with." Yes, there is learning and growing, but it should feel different. How would you feel if church was just like work or just like university studies? Why should it be any different for our kids?

Even if you have a teaching background, the aim is not to try to recreate school. Yes, we all learn about God at church. However, the more important aim at church is to encounter Him, whether we are five or whether we are sixty-five! Perhaps your head has jumped straight to chaos and behaviour management. Take a moment to breathe and don't panic. I'll talk about that in a bit.

Over the years, we have found a change of language to be a very powerful tool for bringing in change. We deliberately moved away from the term "Sunday school" to "kids church." This is because at the heart of it we are coming to church – my husband, my children and I, all of us together. We are not coming to school or work. If we need to define church for the kids differently to the adult church service, then something like "kids church" as a term seems a great declaration of what we are there to do. What we communicate matters, and our heart for the kids in our church is that nothing would hinder them from coming to His house - not their ability to learn or read, nor their background. All that matters is that they would be able to come freely into God's house to praise and worship Him, find out more about Him, encounter Him and be transformed by Him.

I'll talk about the team further on, but if you have some teachers on your team, you can work together to help each other. If you are not a teacher, you can gain skills, gifts and experience from them, but you also need to let them gain your heart and your ministry. Share with them how you would love to get wisdom from their teaching skills. Have conversations about what teaching skills they would consider helpful to bring into kids church. Then share your heart with them. They have already had God give them a heart for kids, and they can now be released to minister to kids in a way in which they are generally not allowed to do in a school setting. If you are a teacher, allow God to give you a freedom and joy that you don't find in the classroom. Ask God for dreams of what He has planned for kids church. Don't just rely on your learnt professionalism and skills. He has far more for them and you than you've ever learnt or known.

How do we care?

You can't pastor a child without pastoring the parent. What affects the one affects the other and vice versa. "What!" you say in sheer panic! "I'm not going to pastor all of the adults also - that's the job of the adults pastor." Breathe and hear me out! To be an effective kids pastor you need a really, really good relationship with the adult leadership team. I'm not talking about the stuff that comes under child protection, we'll deal with that in a separate section, but I am talking about the normal week in week out behaviour and about knowing the kids.

Let's take for example Johnny comes into kids church one week and plays up like crazy. His behaviour's all over the place and the team are frazzled by the end of the service. If you have no reason to believe this is a child protection issue, do you:

a) Hope and pray next week is better.
b) Book to be on holidays next Sunday!
c) Catch up with Johnny's parent after church (or during the week) and ask if Johnny's doing ok because he wasn't his normal self in kids church.

Over the years we have found option c to be so very effective, although I have to admit we never tried option b! It doesn't need to be a big heavy conversation with the parent, just a simple check-in. Often the response we get is – oh yes Johnny wasn't so good on Sunday because we were out late, and he got to bed late on Saturday. Or his friend is giving him a hard time, or .... is going on at home/school. Asking the question does two things. Firstly, it gives you as the kids pastor the opportunity to ask if there's anything particular that kids church can do to support Johnny. Secondly, it gives you the opportunity to ask whether the parent has spoken to the adult leadership to get extra support. That then leads to an easy conversation with the adult leadership team that can put the parent(s) on their radar whilst we as kids team care for the child.

This is a vital part of pastoral care. However, it often gets missed because we are so focussed on the kid's behaviour that we forget the broader context of their lives. Even though you might not see it, what is happening at school or home will affect them, and they need you to help them link the issue and their response to the situation to their relationship with God.

One week, we said to the kids that we were going to pray for just four things and asked what would they like to pray for. Hands shot up! What are the four things you think they wanted to pray for? The first three that they wanted to pray for were their parents, for sick family members, and for friends at school. Yet it was the fourth item that blew our team were away (and brought many close to tears). Three of the kids separately shared that they wanted to pray for their teachers who weren't coping. How wonderful that because of how we approached things in kids church each week, they knew they could bring God, hope and change to their teachers at school.

Likewise, when there is a situation at home, they want to know that God sees them, knows them, loves them and is still holding them and their family. They are reassured that God wants to know about what's happening at home. This is faith being activated in their world.

So don't avoid opportunities to talk to parents and keep those conversations going with the adult leaders. They are precious moments, and you will understand the kids better the more you know the parents. Bear in mind that the kids may show the first signs that something is wrong at home. Please don't shoulder pastoral weight that you're not meant to, but do make sure you pass it on in the right way. Also to note before we move onto the subject of the team. You will find that a lot of your team will be – or certainly should be – parents!!!! So, caring for them as a part of your team is a vital part of your role.

THE PRACTICALITIES

YOUR TEAM

Building teams that are seen

Your team is the most precious resource that you have been given and because kids teams aren't seen in action by much of the church, they need to know that God sees them. They only get to know that when they realise that you see them. It's important you don't just see them when they're not there. See them for who they are, not just what they do. These guys sacrifice time to come and be a part of ministry with you, time they could have spent just resting in God's presence in adult church. This is a precious sacrifice. Receive their offering by noticing them offer it. Don't forget you also need them; believe me you cannot do this role on your own! God wants them not just to be someone who will fill a need. He wants to weave your hearts together. His heart is that you would love them and be built deeper in relationship together as you take ground. That means you need to let them into your heart and over time they will let you into theirs. This doesn't happen overnight. It takes you getting to know them. Ask them what you can pray for, ask after their families, their work, their hearts and their dreams. Know them! Don't just use them.

Guard your team members. Kids church is a place in which people can disappear for years (perhaps that's you too) and they end up never getting into church. Let's be crystal clear – that is NOT healthy nor sustainable for any length of time. Talk with them before you roster them on as to when they come to church (if you have multiple services). If they come to a service each week, then perhaps they could serve on alternate weeks or once every 4 weeks/once a month. The maximum should be fortnightly unless you have several services and they can sit in church for one and serve at the other. If you and your team become disconnected from church that can be half the church that becomes unplugged from the vine. Don't do that. Don't let anyone convince you that it's healthy or that it's your calling to do so. Even nature knows that a parent has to feed themselves to be able to feed their baby. If a team member pitches in to help you on a day that they weren't rostered (and they serve more than once a month) make sure you get someone else to cover their next rostered shift. Cover them, help them guard their hearts so they stay sweet in God's house. Be gentle and kind with them.

In your communication with your team, ask for the Holy Spirit to interpret in such a way that your team are able to hear your heart. We often reduce speaking in tongues and interpretation to some kind of weird utterance that someone gets the translation, but this isn't what it's about at all. It is often called a heavenly language, enabling us to speak heartbeat to heartbeat directly to Heaven. In the same way, in Acts when many heard the disciples speaking, they weren't talking in gibberish, but in a language that enabled them to be understood by others. So very often in church life, our communication is hijacked and misunderstood. This paves the way for hurt and offense, and no more often than within your team. Surely part of the Holy Spirit's work is to continue to enable us, under His empowering, to speak in a way that others can understand, irrespective of the words that we use. I would often pray for my team like this: "God, will you help them to hear my heart, not the words that I speak, and may I hear their heart in return." Don't get upset when someone says something to you that feels like an attack. Ask afresh for the Holy Spirit to help you hear their heart, then we can address any real issues together without getting offended.

In practical ways, speak your team member's language. What do I mean by that? In our modern world, there are many platforms through which to communicate. It can become overwhelming. Often, we say we will communicate everything via a specific channel. For instance, Facebook messenger or Whatsapp. But many people don't use multiple channels. It's powerful when we take notice of who isn't engaging and follow up with them. Ask if that particular communication platform works for them. If it doesn't, build up a list of those to whom you need to send a text instead, or send a text to everyone as well as using the other channels. Taking that care says "I see you, I see that you are not engaging, it matters to me that you do engage and I value you to that level. How can I make it easier for you?" – your team will love you for it.

Knotty team stuff

So here we get to the first of the knotty elements - you! You are running kids church each week and you're not getting into the main church service. It needs to change, but how? Let's be real, it won't magically change overnight, but you can make a plan to start changing it. While you can raise up an oversight team to cover you when you're on holidays or off sick, they should also cover you regularly so that you can get into church. It's good for you, but it's also good for them, as it means they're more practiced for when you are on holidays or if you're sick. Moreover, it shows them you trust them. Please don't make a change overnight and leg it! Start to establish them, tell your team what the overseers will be doing, and mentor the overseers. Get them to shadow you once a month or once each fortnight, make sure they get introduced to the team if they don't know everyone. Pray together with them, share your heart with them and then start to let them oversee a single service with you in church (but with your phone on, so they can call you should they need to). Chat with them afterwards. Start small, even if one person can cover you once a month that's a start, build from there. It can be different, and it must be different for you to be able to run the distance of the race God has given you.

Who should be on our team?

As far as I'm concerned it is simple. If you put your child in the programme, then you need to serve one service once a month. That's the bottom line. If we are trying to build our team by waiting for people in church to discover that their calling is kids church, we're in trouble! It is not unreasonable to expect parents to do at least one shift, once a month on the team if their child is in the kids programme. There is no magic fairy that looks after the children. It is volunteers who all pitch in to make it happen. So with your minister's permission put a communication out to all parents explaining that to be able to have enough people on the team, every parent needs to do one shift then the need would be covered. The only parents I exclude from that expectation are the ones who serve heavily in other areas of church life. If there are people going through a traumatic time in life then I may suggest a break, because I know and love them. However, sometimes their time on the kids church roster can be just what God uses to bring life and hope and joy back into their world. Have the conversation with them. When you genuinely care for your team, they will follow your heart anywhere.

Whilst getting commitment from parents is a starting point, make sure that you also engage young adults, older folks and grandparents. The kids need young adults to be energetic and fun, to be people they look up to and want to be like when they're older. They also need grandparent figures to dote on them and spend time with them, listening to them and being interested in them.

Also consider asking anyone who's tried to give you ideas and suggestions on how to improve kids church! If they've got ideas and they're not on the team, then tell them how awesome their idea is (assuming that it is) and let them know you need them on the team to help build kids church. God's obviously given them a heart and creative ideas for this, and perhaps being on the team will give them a greater understanding of the challenges that you face. They may understand your rationale for doing some of the things you do, and are likely to then become some of your strongest supporters and encouragers.

There is one other section of people who are absolutely vital in your team – older kids. "What!" you cry "they don't fill my ratio!" Not yet they won't, but they will be the BEST and most trained team members when they become adults. We have raised kids up from age twelve and cared for them, encouraged them and trained them over the years. By the time they hit 18, they are already trained and capable to take full responsibility and lead a room. If you are getting no response from your young adults right now, then you need to play the long game and raise up your twelve-year-olds so that within six years (yes this is strategic!) you'll have some amazing young adults on your team! However, something else happens when you have older kids on your team. The younger ones will imitate them and follow their example. We have seen our older kids on our team settle the most tricky of two-year-olds in a heart-beat. They become like big brothers and sisters to the kids in kids church.

When you have all the generations on your kids team, you will have the strongest team possible and the kids will thrive through the rich interactions.

Who should not be on your team?

So that's who you should have on your team. However, there are a few sets of folks you should not have on your team – I told you this stuff can get a bit knotty! Whatever you do, make sure you follow your church's onboarding process, as it is there for a reason. We want kids church to be many things – a place of encounter with God and loving and fun, but if it is not safe you cannot do any of those things. We absolutely have to ensure that we have done everything in our power to make kids church the safest place in the world. I know many of the checks for onboarding are about whether they have a criminal record. In Queensland, that's the blue card checks. However, this is only the start. You might also doublecheck with adult leadership to ensure they have no safety concerns. Personally, I've also tended to ask leadership if the person has a particular problem with lying. Why is that? Because, if they struggle to tell the truth in a repeated pattern, how can you trust their account of anything in the room?

Who else should not be on your team? Anyone who's been doing it for years and is DONE! Sometimes what started as a joy is now not even a duty, it's a heavy, heavy weight upon their shoulders. Set them free to explore other areas of church life! Encourage them to rest if they need to for a *little* time. Then they can go try some other area of church life and find enjoyment there! If you can, keep checking in on them and see how they're going in their new role. Sometimes they then rediscover the joy and return to kids church.

A "pitch in together" culture

Establishing an expectation of reciprocity on the team is vital. This means that if a team member can't make their shift and someone has covered for them, they are expected to cover someone else's shift. Let's be honest, life happens, so rostering is not going to work if it's a static, immovable spreadsheet. We may get sick, our kids get sick, we have holidays, we have family visiting. Rosters should be flexible. Your team should know it is fine to block a date out, or swap last minute if required. However, you need to ensure you set an expectation that if someone cannot do this week, they will need to cover a shift next week or the week after. That they understand that you have had to pull someone from next week to fill their slot. Therefore they need to do next week or the week after in return. When "we pitch in together" it reiterates each team members' value and their commitment to you and the whole team. Setting this expectation reminds everyone that they are not just an addition, but that you truly rely on them. If you are crumbling because your team just does not turn up, you need to talk with them individually and kindly (not accusingly). Ask questions like, "Is everything OK? You seem to be missing roster a lot" with the goal to help them understand they are needed and important in the team. However, you might have to have a gentle conversation that helps them understand that if they don't make a roster, there are implications. Either a room has to be shut and kids don't get kids church, or someone has to step in, which might have other impacts on that person. These conversations may sound daunting but they will provide great strength of relationship moving forward.

Let's return to simplifying rostering for your team. Can I suggest you do use one of the technology solutions which are available. These platforms take into account the flexibility of life, by enabling people to block out holiday dates, surgery dates and any other planned dates. This makes it easier for our precious team to communicate with you when they are not available.

Making their roster work for them respects their time and other commitments, which increases their buy-in to the team.

One other point on rostering. Send rosters out in advance. Everyone is wired differently; some people are master planners but some deal week by week. You need to roster so that both are given what they need to succeed. We have found that sending rosters out three months ahead meant that those on our team who plan ahead can lock dates in. Our technology platform would send an email at that initial point communicating the roster shifts. Then we set our technology platform to then email a reminder of that roster one week ahead and we would send a text/messenger/whatsapp. If you have a team member who repeatedly does not turn up on the roster and seems confused when you ask why they missed their roster, I suggest you go back to basics. Check the simple things like whether you have the right email address and phone number. Ask whether the emails are going into their spam/junk folder etc. We had a fabulous team member who kept missing rosters. It took almost a year to realise we had the wrong email address AND the wrong phone number! Checking the simple things make all the difference. You may find out that the team member is simply disorganised. If that's the case chat with them about the best way to communicate with them, how can you help them? That again reinforces that you want them on the team and that you want to make it easy for them to be so.

Training

When you love your team, you want to equip them, enable them to be more effective, and help and support them in their role. We typically did training sessions four times a year in person, with a Zoom option. These sessions were also recorded and a YouTube section created which allowed all of the team to access any sessions they might have missed or wanted to rewatch. Over the years these training videos became such a helpful treasure where we could refer a team member to if they were wanting help in a particular area. These sessions were normally around 1.5 hours in length.

The most effective start to a training session was always to ask for feedback from the team. This gave them a fresh opportunity to review things from their point of view and would air frustrations quickly so they did not build up. It would also give us as leadership a far clearer idea as to where things actually were at on the ground. This feedback was also used to shape the content of the next training session.

Training should cover practicalities which span distinct topics, such as:

- How to engage kids in praise and worship
- How to read a story in engaging ways (This might cover specific areas like how to use your voice, props, or drama. Each of which can be a 15 min section in their own right)
- How to setup the room
- How to deal with behaviour management
- What to do in emergency situations (you don't want them fearful of 'what if')
- How to pray with small ones
- How to project your voice (I suggest asking someone from the music team or experienced public speakers to teach this).

You don't have to be the one doing all the training. You might have someone on your team who is great at getting the kids talking over morning tea. Ask them if they would do part or all of a 15-minute session. This is also a great encouragement for a team member that you have noticed how they are great at that particular element to the point that they are able to help others. What a joy to encourage them in that way! Normally we would talk for 10-15 minutes and then allow a further 5-10 minutes for questions.

The final part of the meeting would be impartation. Praying for your team, imparting to them is essential. We would normally do this in the last half an hour. As well as their ministry in kids church, your team members are people with families, work, life challenges, dreams. Know those things and pray with them for those parts of their world.

When your team know you want to equip them to succeed in kids team, they will feel supported in that.

NOBODY PANIC!

When none of your plans have come to pass on a morning, it's a gravy day! It's those days when everything you planned has gone to gravy! Remember there will always be those days, but as you build your team you can build resilience into that team. Roster on one extra person more than your ratio requires (or two, dependent upon the size of your team). Alternatively, you might have a position on the roster that is emergency help, so that when you have half of your team all down sick (it happens) you know where you can start to pull people in. I built up an emergency list of people who didn't want to be on a regular roster for various and justifiable reasons but were happy to be messaged the day before or the morning of if there was a last-minute need. Be honest, you can only be in one place at a time. You cannot singlehandedly cover all the ratios. You need to know who you can call on for emergency help.

Then rest

"What!!!" you say! I know that I just talked about gravy days, but guys let's be real, sometimes even with a backup plan you still cannot cover ratio, and you may have to limit or even close a room. This is never the first go to, it is the last resort. Yet, when you have offered all you have and juggled all you can, you have to be at peace. You may not have anyone say well done in that moment, but rest knowing that you did everything you could to make it happen. Just make sure that you communicate that with your leadership. They are there for your covering, and they need to know if you were not able to fulfil a full complement of rooms, especially if it becomes a recurring situation.

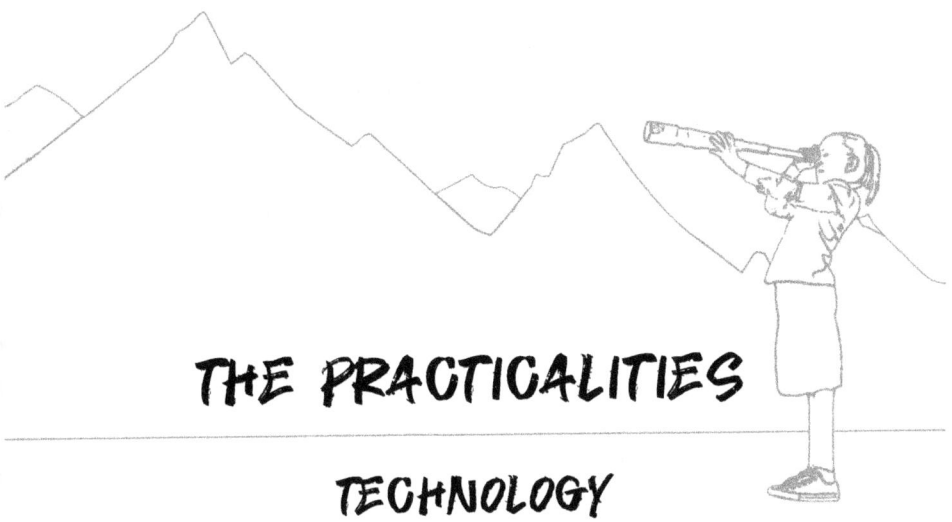

THE PRACTICALITIES

TECHNOLOGY

Play to your strengths

OK who groaned when they read this title? Yes, me too! I am not technical. Technology frustrates me like crazy. However, my husband is technical, as is my son and my daughter (yes we have served in kids church as family together for many years). So play to your strengths. You may have a few of the regular older kids to whom you can give a little training and responsibility. They could make things work technology-wise for you week-on-week. Talk with their parents and see if they think the child is ready for that, then set out your expectation with them.

You can't abdicate responsibility however. You will need to know how to use any technology that is implemented. If you're starting from scratch, get someone with technical understanding to help establish some foundations, even if they are not on the kids team. Technology should help and not hinder what you do. It should make the work easier not harder. And whatever you do don't change it just for the sake of changing it.

There are a number of areas where technology can be a wonderful help:

1. Rostering. As I mentioned earlier, there are some great, simple products out there that make rostering very easy from your team's side and are not difficult to manage. If you have a small team of two or three rostered on each week, then you probably don't need a rostering system. Once you get to a team of 20 or more, trying to keep track of who's doing what and when gets much trickier. There may be a tool that other areas of your church use – perhaps the music team are already using a system and it works well. Don't reinvent the wheel just for the sake of it. It will cost your church extra for a different solution. If you can use

the same tool as other areas of church life, things stay more streamlined across the whole church.

2. Kids check-in. It is vital to work within your child safety policies and practices to ensure that your check-in and check-out practices are safe, workable and effective. We can have the best policy, but if it's too hard in practice, then it's ineffective. Complex check in systems can be challenging when your team have got big groups of parents collecting their kids. Ideally, the system should be linked in with your main church database to eliminate double ups in the data resulting in extra administration. Check-in labels are incredibly useful in many ways. They help the team learn names, know at a glance any food allergies, and if used in duplicate (one label goes on the child, one label the parent keeps) they ensure adults are the perfect method at check-out to show the person has the authorisation to collect the child. This might not be such a big issue in a small church but in big churches, your team won't necessarily know all the parents, nor will they necessarily know if there are domestic/legal orders in place. This is where a check-in label is a wonderful tool, providing authorisation around who can collect each child. No adult label at check-out

means there's no authorisation, and therefore no collection of the child. We'll talk more about this later on.

3. Amplification. Again, this will depend upon the size of your room(s), but when you have a lot of kids in a room you don't want your team to feel like they're having to shout over the noise all the time - that simply escalates the sound. Yes, some of your team may be able to project their voices, but many won't have this skill. So, you have a choice, you can either train them to be able to project or recognise that many don't. In this case some amplification is helpful. A simple microphone for the room leader can make all the difference. It keeps the sound in the room at talking level, rather than it being perceived as shouting. This in turn keeps the sense of peace within a room. If you have the privilege of live musicians leading praise and worship, you may want a bigger setup. However, be mindful that simplicity is key. Ensure that amplification tools are easy for all team members to use, this avoids frustration and challenges when the technology does not work.

4. Programming. There are some incredible media resources out there that can be used in the context of a service programme. Hear me right, I'm not saying just put the

media on for the duration of your time in kids church, but if there's a few-minute snippet that emphasises the theme for the day, use it! To do so, you will need to have a setup that will make this easy. Gone are the days of buying a DVD and putting that into a DVD/TV combo! In your planning, think about the best way to view the media, and ask your team for help. You're not being a burden; God has given each of your team members different spiritual and natural gifts. They are a part of His provision to you and kids church, so give them opportunity help.

Some final advice with technology. Don't ever let the technology drive what you do. It underpins and enables, but should not dictate. And remember, whatever you do, don't change technology just for the sake of changing it. If it ain't broke... don't fix it!

THE PRACTICALITIES

PROGRAMME STRUCTURE

So, what should you include in a programme? Every church is different and every kids church is different. There are different seasons. Different leaders lead in different ways with different skills. That's OK. This is not about a one size fits all, but it is about ensuring the right elements are in place.

One factor to consider is the time your kids church starts. Do parents drop the kids off before the adult service begins? Or is it after worship? How long is your adult service? In some churches there isn't a regular answer to that question! The amount of time you have will affect what you can put in the programme.

My template for kids church is based on the normal adult church service – but each church will have certain things in different orders, so do what you would normally do with the adults, ensuring there's enough variation to keep the kids engaged. Surely we should have similar elements to the adult service, albeit with different expressions. So, what are the main elements in an adult service?

Praise and worship

If kids stay in the adult service during the time of praise and worship, then there's probably no need to do further praise and worship separately. However, if the kids are out in kids church from the beginning of service, it is important to start with praise and worship. If you are privileged enough to have team members who are skilled musicians and can provide live praise and worship, you are blessed indeed! Enjoy! However, if you need to use media to sing along, don't beat yourself up or worry about it. Encourage the kids to praise God with everything they have.

When you are choosing songs, remember that until about the age of six or seven, putting words up on the screen is not helpful. The kids are unlikely to be capable of reading at that pace! If the aim is to enable kids to enter into the presence of God, then make it easy for them to do so at their specific developmental stage. Choose songs that are repetitive with lots of movement/active expression rather than songs that are very wordy.

In addition to singing, you can engage younger aged kids with instruments like drums, maracas, and toy guitars. Also, you can have ribbons or pieces of sheer material to wave. Lots of children LOVE to dance, so whether working with old or young kids, these are great elements. Train the team that all they need to do is just need lead the way and be ready and expectant to come into God's presence!

There will be the odd occasion when the kids are just flat or distracted. If it's not happening, take a moment to stop, pray, and if they are school age then lightly and gently remind the kids that they have an invitation from God who loves them so, so, so very much to come into His presence. God knew they would be there today, and He's been waiting and looking forward to this moment. They're not there because someone brought them, but because God Himself wanted them here. You can then help them get moving – do some jumping jacks, running on the spot, anything that gets them ready to praise.

Again, when it is time to worship, it is worth pausing rather than continuing to just sing and stop for a moment to pray. They might want different options through which to express their worship. Perhaps they need to focus, and it will help to close their eyes and raise their hands. Maybe kneeling or lying on the floor is a better option - although it's sometimes hard to get them back up again!

Notices/Updates about church life

If we start to believe and understand that our kids are PART of the church, then when something new is happening in the life of the church we want to include them and make sure that they know. This could be a building project commencing, a mission day or a vision day. Let the kids know! If your church produces media about it, ask to be able to show it to the kids in kids church. If there are pictures of a new part of the building planned, then show them those. If there are people doing something new, tell them. Why? Because that connects them in with the wholeness of church. They might want to have their own building fund offering (see below). At the very least, they can pray for new leaders or pray for the new vision. Remember their prayers hit heaven the same way that ours do.

Offering

This is an important element because we are giving the kids the opportunity to express their hearts. We give to that which we love, and the Bible tells us that where our treasure is, there our heart will be also (Matt 6:21). Having an offering gives kids an opportunity to express how much they value their church, and it establishes Godly principles in their world. So how do the practicalities work around that? Take your lead from what your church does. Kids church is not separate to the house of God, it is a part of it. To save counting up money each week, you might want to create a big money box that is unopenable without a screwdriver. Then it can be opened once every six months for counting. You can let the kids know that this was counting week and then tell them the following week how much they have given as our part of church.

If it has not been a regular part of your programme, I suggest talking to leadership and with their agreement, then with the parents before implementing an offering segment. Then discuss with the kids what offering is and why you are doing it in kids church.

Assuming that you are ready to implement it, keep the segment short within your programme. Perhaps in the weeks leading up to it your messages could be around the topic of giving into the house of God. Then in the following weeks, just take a short moment to speak on offering. You could ask the kids themselves why we give and choose a different child each week to answer. Complete the segment by praying together for your church and then let the kids give. It doesn't need to be more complex than that.

If you have a specific building fund day, talk about the plans in the days leading up to it and get the kids excited for the future of the church. They might want to do something to raise money such as a car wash. You will find you'll have a lot of enthusiasm on your hands, which will in turn excite others in church.

Message

How you do the message section will depend upon the age of the kids in the room. Don't reinvent the wheel! There are many preplanned resources which you can use, so don't be afraid to use them. However, you do have freedom to be creative. Just watch your time, don't labour the message, keep it time appropriate for the age of kids you've got - it still needs to be fun!

With younger kids, you might read the Bible story and then talk about it over morning tea. However, if the passage is one where you can get them involved then go for it! For example, with something like Jonah and the whale, get a big tent and pretend it is the whale and get all the kids in it (safely!). Or if it's Jericho, march around big cardboard boxes and yell and have the boxes fall down (safely!). You might have someone on your team who's really good with puppets or craft. You can make masks to be the characters in the story. Being a storyteller is such a powerful gift in kids church - there are many, many wonderful ways of telling a story. It isn't just about retelling the crossing of the red sea, it could also be the foundation for sharing a testimony. When you are a storyteller, you invite others to join you in immersing themselves in the story. When this is paired with God's power, it is an incredibly transformative skill through which the Holy Spirit can move powerfully.

With older kids you might use drama or some other kind of media or simply read a Bible passage. Again, you can give them parts of a story. They could be different characters and have words to read while one of the kids themselves read the Scripture. Wherever they can be involved make it happen! Providing kids with the opportunity to ask questions and come to grips with how it applies to them is really important.

With older kids, you also need to ensure there is enough time to unpack the message. Small group times are the perfect forum for having a chat and allowing the kids to ask questions. It is in that smaller setting they can learn how to grasp and apply what they've heard. If you have members of team who are just a few years older, they might be up for leading a small group. Again, there are many ideas of how to do this. We did a term about different ways to hear from God. Each child was given a journal and we made space after each message for them to write down what God spoke to them. In another term, kids took home part of a puzzle, which acted as a visual prompt to remind them of how they can apply scripture.

Appeal

Yes, you read this right! For older kids (five years and up), it is wonderful to give them an opportunity to respond for salvation. Going back to what I talked about in the heart section, kids do not need to be able to theologically explain their standpoint about the end times to make a simple response to say yes to Jesus. He is looking for their hearts. Who are we to deny them that opportunity? They should get the same opportunity that the adults get. It is truly the biggest decision they will ever make.

Don't be put off if the same kids respond each week. We've had many conversations over the years with adults on team who struggle with this, but it is the most beautiful thing, and I truly believe that we as adults have something incredible to gain from their approach. You see we are meant to continue throughout our lives to encounter Jesus afresh and in response say yes to Him. When we follow the kids' example we get greater revelation of this truth. I have discovered that in one appeal they might say yes to having Jesus in their heart, the next appeal they might say yes to having Jesus as their friend, the following one they might realise He is their rescuer, and then next they might understand that they can be a child of God. Why do we limit our salvation to one decision and then maybe a rededication moment? God wants us to ongoingly be born again, and again and again (John 3:7)!!! Follow the kids' example – keep saying yes to Jesus!

The appeal time also gives the kids an opportunity to respond to and engage with the message. This might not be through verbal prayer; it might be action-based. For instance, they might write down something God challenged them to get rid of and put it in a big bin. They might write a dream and make it into a paper airplane and "send it up to God" in flight. They might draw what God has shown them. There are many ways to engage kids in their response, but it is important that they have that opportunity for a heart response.

Memory Verses

You might think this is old school! Well perhaps it is a bit. Yet time and time again, we have seen the value of learning scripture. We talk a lot with our team about "anchors for the soul." Our prayer is that by establishing learnt Scripture in their hearts, these Scriptures would hold them fast, even when everything in their world is shaking. Scriptures that kids learn will become anchors that hold them not just when they're little, not just in school, but throughout their life. Those same truths will be anchors in their teens when everything changes. And in their twenties, when they make big life decisions. The anchors of truth will continue to direct them in their thirties and beyond. When their world shakes, that truth will be their rock and fortress. Whether Scripture is learnt through song or through memory verse, I know for a fact that over the years my anchors have held me in the darkest of times. It is what I've leaned on; what I've clung onto.

So how do you do it? A few simple principles:

- Make it an age-appropriate length.
- Add actions to reinforce the words (one time we made foam "lily pads" that they had to jump on to remember the word).
- Keep the same memory verse for a term so it is repeated many times.
- Have prizes for those who can remember the verse at the end of term.
- Have it on the wall to help the team!

Activities

Activities are wonderfully fun ways to reinforce a message. Before I go further, let's just clarify that an activity doesn't need to be craft!!! It can be things like a no-bake cooking or a treasure hunt. If you've talked about sin and falling short of the mark, you can use the soft dart boards (Velcro only - don't give kids sharp darts!). If you've talked about how God made you, reinforce that concept with clay or playdough. Yes, there are hundreds of crafts to match all sorts of themes, but it does not stop there. You will find that you will engage different children by offering a variety of activities.

Fellowship

It's important that the kids have the opportunity to just be together. We found at one point that whilst we had an amazing kids church service, there was no space for the kids to just hang out together and so they didn't really know each other. Once we realised this was an issue, we worked hard to change our service pattern so that there was space for the kids to have a time of fellowship. As a part of group work with older kids we often had hang out time, where the kids played card games, or other simple games they could play whilst hanging out and chatting. If you've got an outdoor play area, consider taking groups of kids outside either midway through or at the end of the main service. Have different play options available - soccer, handball, bowling, hula hoops, chalk board, hopscotch. There are so many options, although it always depends on the space that you have available. One couple we helped were heading up kids church in their venue which was a cinema. Sure, this created some interesting dynamics for kids' play, but even in that situation there were a number of games we came up with that the kids loved.

Why is fellowship through play so important? Because we want to enable them to develop life-giving friendships. At the older ages especially, their friendships in church can be a part of carrying them well through their teenage years. Even though some of the friendships might change, to have them used to being established with friendship in the house of God will help them through those slightly awkward or difficult years.

Morning tea

There are practical reasons to include morning tea in kids church, but it will depend upon how long the kids are with you. If you're looking at a service time of 1.5 hours, you will need to give the kids something to eat during that time. Otherwise, they will be so hungry they'll be distracted anyway. However, there's a greater reason to doing morning tea in kids church than mere necessity.

Jesus often ate with people, and it was whilst eating food that He shared His heart. If it was good enough for Jesus, I reckon we should do the same!

Eating food together, no matter how simple, gives folks a time to know and be known. You can chat about the message, find out how their week has been - it's a very powerful time for the team to engage with the kids. If you're wondering about allergies, you'll be pleased to know that we will cover some of the practicalities on how to do morning tea in a bit.

Games

We've often used team games as fun start and finish points. You don't need big spaces for all game types, nor do you need lots of expensive equipment. Games are also useful if a service runs longer than you expected. Create a folder that includes a whole range of different game resources and instructions. That way, when you've suddenly got an extra half an hour your team aren't struggling for something to do. Instead, they can just grab the folder and have got an easy load of extra things they can do.

THE PRACTICALITIES

THE TRICKY BITS

If you haven't guessed by now, there is no topic off limits here. My heart is that your confidence will extend beyond what to do, to include how to go about it. So here come the "big ticket" things - the areas that probably cause you the most concern within kids church - and a whole load of hints and tips to navigate them well.

Are you ready? ☺

Child safety - policy & practice.

You need to know your child safety/protection policy. It is vital for you to know what the church requires of you and the team with regards child safety.

If your church does not have a child safety/protection policy then you need to discuss this with your leadership. We cannot be effective in any way if we don't put the safety of our kids first. Do make sure that your policy is practical. Policy documents become useless when they are unrealistic or unworkable for the team to do. This isn't just in the church arena, it's the same in the workplace. Having worked in business as an auditor, I know from experience that employees will totally ignore an unworkable policy. If there is something in your policy that isn't clear or is impractical, then put forward a suitable alternative and request a change to the policy.

We had a large team, so we created a second document which specified team practice based upon the policy. That meant that although four of us knew the policy inside out, when it came to the team, we only trained them on what was required in practice. In short, this meant they learnt the policy via the practice we taught. Let's be real, most of your team will not want to read a policy document, nor should they need to. Make it easy for them to comply with policy by training them on safety practices.

One of the key child safety areas involves the checking in and checking out or collection of children. The most vital thing is not whether it involves technology, it is whether it is simple and safe. A simple process ensures that every child is returned to the right adult. This is easier in a smaller church setting where parents are known, but even then issues can arise. Custody or domestic issues are confidential and therefore will only be known to a few people. However, this confidentiality can leave a gap in knowledge which may lead to a serious incident. It is crucial that we guard our beautiful children - no one wants our church to get caught in the fallout, and a potential parental wrangle over custody. Keep it simple! Whatever the delivering adult gets given at drop off is what needs to returned in order for the child to be released. It is the cleanest, simplest way to guarantee that the person collecting is indeed authorised to collect the child. If you think these scenarios don't happen, I'm sorry to tell you they do. Please believe me when I tell you that following your approved process will ensure that the right outcomes happen afterwards.

Ratios

You need to know your ratios.

Once again, they should be super simple. Typically, there is an under-three-year-old ratio and an over-three-year-old ratio. However, the legal requirements for supervision will vary dependent upon where in the world you are. Make sure that your team know their ratios. We did this simply by putting up the ratios in the room on a sign and training the team as to why they matter.

Extra hint: This is where an under-18 team member helps. While they don't technically support the ratio, they can be considered to cover your policy requirement to always have two team members in the room. As long as the under-18 team member is of an age to be truthful and can tell a truthful account, then our policy always allowed for us to have one adult team member and one under-18 and keep to ratio for that one adult. It's very helpful. However, do check for what your policy allows and stay aligned.

Fire drills

You need to know your emergency assembly points and your team need to know them also. It would be the worst thing out to not be able to evacuate a kids room. So practice! It doesn't have to be a hard or scary thing, just a regular practice - every six months or so. Keep it simple and find out what your team don't know. This is not so that you beat them with a stick, but so that you know in advance, as opposed to finding it out during an actual emergency. It also ensures the kids are used to doing fire drills, and know what to do and where to go. At one point there were a couple of false alarms at our church. It was truly wonderful to see the kids and kids team leading the way to the evacuation points, because they knew and practiced them regularly!

Do identify rooms that might be hard to evacuate and address the risks. Examples of that would be an under 3s room up a set of stairs. There can be simple solutions that might involve members of other teams coming to help that room evacuate. All of that needs to be risk assessed, communicated and practiced.

You don't need an alarm to do a fire drill. Just let the team know you'll be doing fire drills over the coming weeks. On the day, walk into the room and say (nice and calmly) that this is the fire drill, and then let your team take over.

Extra hint: Put a sign on the door of the room you are evacuating so that any parents who are coming to check on their kids don't freak out that all the kids have disappeared! Yes, we learnt that one the hard way!

Food

We've already talked about how morning tea is a wonderful way to engage kids. However, when dealing with kids it is vital that we do this right, so we don't put any child at risk.

Addressing allergies is the first step. When a child is signed in on their first visit, the parent should document whether a child has food allergies. Our check-in system enabled allergies to be one of the lines printed onto each kids' check-in label. This was helpful for the rotating team, who could easily have a visual on any allergies.

The simplest way to enable morning tea is to have food in the room that is rarely an issue for allergies – rice crackers and dried fruit are normally pretty safe. If you want to offer other food, then know both the cost and assess potential allergy risks.

One great tip for having a visual on allergies are the disposable wristbands. Especially if you have new or rotating teams that won't know all the kids nor their allergies. Also, if we were going to have specific food items in a room, for example cornflakes for sensory play, then we would put a large poster on the door where the parents enter with the kids. "Today we will be using cornflakes in our play. If your child is allergic, please notify the team on arrival." This again underpins the working together between parents and the team.

A tricky one to navigate can be children bringing their own food into the room. You can address this in a few ways. One simple very straight forward approach is to not allow anyone to bring their own food into the room. Especially with the younger years, this approach ensures no one grabs someone else's food and eats it (there's not just allergy concerns with that!). It also brings a togetherness where kids are all sharing the same food and there's no jealousy. Alternatively, you can address it by ensuring labelling of lunch boxes and close supervision of kids as they eat. However, this can be hard to police when there's a lot of kids. Considering the breadth of identified allergies now, this increases the likelihood that there would be foods that would cause another child an allergic reaction in the room. The knowledge for this potential risk can make the team very nervous and understandably so. Remember our kids are precious and so is our team! We want to keep kids safe but also make keeping the kids safe as easy as possible for the team. There have been times when we have struggled just to have the water bottles labelled at times, let alone a lunchbox! You do need to be aware to never underestimate the child who is being "helpful" and feeding another child their food – it happens!

Behaviour Management

Many studies have shown that when a child knows their boundaries, they feel safe. Indeed, if we think about ourselves even as adults, we feel safer or more at peace when we have clarity on expectations. Having fun does not mean there is no behaviour management and that absolute chaos is needed to have fun. Think about how many times a game becomes not fun when there's no clarity around the rules. The expectations are different for behaviour dependent upon age, but the boundaries can remain consistent. Again, each team member will be great at different ways of engaging kids. Let's work through how we used to structure the placement of our team in a room:

1. Always have a leader at the front who drives the flow of the programme. They are not the one who will deal with a lot of behaviour issues. Their role is to keep the majority of the kids engaged and going in the same direction. This person will be able to read the ebbs and flow of the room and direct the kids accordingly. Often these team members will be confident and energetic personalities.

2. Next, dependent upon how many team and kids you have in the room, you need assign some team who are "scoopers." As the leader leads from the front, the scoopers scoop along the back and draw the kids forward. These team members will be great encouragers, they will build up the shy ones, comfort the scared ones, and focus those who are easily distracted.

3. If you have a lot of kids and a bigger team, then other team members can be positioned strategically in the front row of kids to set an example and through the middle to maintain awareness of what's going on.

4. Whether at the front, back or middle, every team member should be involved with the kids in the programme. If there's preparation of morning tea to be done, it's helpful to either do it ahead of time or get the kids themselves to help distribute it if old enough. None of the team are to disengage, otherwise what does that communicate to the kids – that they are not worth your attention?

5. To establish a positive culture in school age kids you might adopt a kids' code. Something like – we listen, we love, we light up! Repeat it each week and add positive reinforcement for those doing it. Positive reinforcement can come in a number of ways. You could have a prize box, or tickets/stickers that build towards a prize. Endeavouring to establish a culture of catching them doing the right thing works incredibly well. You can also bring in tribes where they are grouped and working/learning together, so that their peers will also help encourage great choices and right behaviours.

This sets up your positive and proactive behaviour management and gets the 99% going in the right direction and doing the right thing.

What about the 1%? Well remember again, we love and want to support our team, and we want our kids to know we love them too. These are the two aims of our communication when it comes to addressing behaviour that isn't right/safe. Whatever strategies you decide to adopt please can I encourage you to get the teams to be consistent in their behavioural expectations. Then the kids will know the expectation and exactly what will happen when behaviour is not acceptable.

Over the years we have found a clear 3-step process works amazingly well:

1. Identify the incorrect behaviour with the child. Tell them it's not acceptable in kids church and that you're expecting that they'll not do that again. Please don't overdo the communication, the child will switch off. A one line explaining this is the behaviour that is not acceptable, please do not do it again is quite sufficient.

2. Should the behaviour reoccur, use a firmer (not harsh) tone and reiterate that the behaviour is not acceptable and that they need to change their behaviour as it is not OK. Let them know that if they don't change you will have to contact their parent and they will have to go back in the service, which you don't want to do because you love having them in kids church. This gives them the encouragement to change because they want to stay in. It also sets the consequences out clearly.

3. The final and third step is to say that they haven't made a great choice and you're very sad that they've not changed their behaviour so you will now contact their parents as you said you would. Ensure they and the parents know that it's just the behaviour that wasn't ok, and you're very much looking forward to them making amazing choices and having a great time together next week. Note that I have not said the fifth, sixth or seventh occasion? Three is final, because otherwise your team will get frustrated. Moreover, kids will know that you will not follow through on what you say. Consistency of response reinforces the behaviour boundaries clearly.

You can be firm in the above, but there's no need to shout unless someone is in danger. Stay calm, and stick to a clear process. It is rarely appropriate to have the above conversations in front of the whole group, so speak to a child individually. This is why the team need to be amongst the children helping them engage. When they are with the children, they can have the quiet but firm conversation if needed.

There may be times when your team aren't able to keep the three step warning consistent. For example, often in the run up to Christmas there is just too much excitement. As the one with full responsibility for kids church, it may take you stepping in and redrawing the boundaries for EVERYONE to hear! We have done this very successfully by role playing in front of the whole group. It involved one team member acting as the child not doing the right thing, and the other team member pretending to be one of the team who is following the step-by-step process. This type of role play sets a clear expectation for both the kids and the team and is a great reset button for all involved.

A highly effective technique to move a child on from a behaviour is to connect and redirect. First get the child's attention by using their name, this communicates that you see them. Then redirect them to the next thing, a positive thing, for example let's go and build some lego. Movement from one place to another (from the hand ball to the lego) helps a child move on from the behaviour and start afresh. Sometimes you can't physically encourage movement from one place to another but from one kind of movement (kicking the child next to them) to another (dancing in praise). The sense of movement, being seen, and an encouragement to not miss out all work wonderfully together to redirect away from behaviour that you don't want. Even as adults we can get stuck and these three keys can also help us get out of our heads, away from negativity and back on the move.

If a regular pattern of unacceptable behaviour starts to occur, please review your processes and chat with parents. It could be a simple thing - perhaps the child is one of the eldest in the group and they've become bored. If so, maybe they could be more of a helper to you and take some (age appropriate) responsibility in the room. Bored kids can misbehave, so address the root issue first. However, it could also be a cry for help or attention. If a child has learnt that certain behaviour gets attention, then spend time with them and focus on verbally affirm them when they're doing the right things. This shows that you see them and that you're really glad they've come today, which will bring changes to their behaviour long term.

Communication to parents

Communication with parents is absolutely vital, but not just when addressing negative issues. If you can, take the parents on the journey with you. Have them as part of your team, get their buy-in to what God's called you and the team to do. It will make your work so much easier in the long term.

If there is lack of communication then parents will read between the lines or make assumptions. They may even leave church over something you will be totally unaware of. As parents, our children are very precious, rightly so! This means that if something happens with a child, their parent needs to know who to talk to AND that you want to have that conversation. They need to know that you are approachable and that you genuinely care for their child. Initiating the tough conversations will avoid frustration building up in a parent and you. If something has happened during the programme, wherever possible talk to the parent that day. If a team member tells you they weren't sure how a parent took something they said, make sure you initiate and follow up with the parent. Proactive communication may very well nip any potential issues in the bud.

The flip side is that if you can consistently get great communication going, then you will also have parents approach you not just when something has gone wrong but also when amazing things are happening in their kids. They will be so much more supportive when they see God has touched their child. They are more likely to tell you when their child's prayer life changes or how hard their child worked to remember the memory verse... What joy is that!!! Treasure those precious moments, for they are part of God's gift to you as a reward for what you do. It also helps to remind you, in the midst of the whirlwind, why you are doing what you're doing.

How to communicate to parents?

So how do you communicate? We have used multiple channels and options over the years. For a long time we did a monthly newsletter which was effective. Although it might waste some paper, it definitely got the updates directly into parents' hands. Our newsletters would cover things like the theme for the term and the memory verse, along with practical things like seasonal reminders. For instance: please ensure you send your child in with a named water bottle and don't forget to put sunscreen on your child before sending them into kids church.

If you are wondering why we didn't email the communication, it has been proven that a high percentage of people never read emails (studies show between 55-74%). This can mean that as leaders, we assume that we've communicated, but the parents have not received the communication.

If there is something serious, such as a safety announcement or important like an event, we would email and text all parents. This double hit approach has proven successful over the years.

It's also important that you routinely check contact details, including kids health updates and emergency numbers. There is nothing worse than an emergency occurring when you do not have the correct phone number for the parent. Some parents can get put off about data updates, but when you explain that it is for the purpose of keeping kids safe, they understand.

When the parents hear from you regularly about your heart for God, your heart for their kids, your heart for what you want

God to do in their kids, then simple things like this become much easier.

Budget and Resources

We have many incredible resources for kids in this generation - games, activity play, sensory play, technology. However, before you go running off to the shops, please stop for a minute! You need to check two important things:

1.   Do you have a budget for kids church?
2.   Where will you store it?

First things first, do you have a budget?

If not, this is the moment to have that conversation with your senior leadership. To be entrusted with a church budget is an incredible privilege and one we don't take lightly. We need to maximise any resource we are given and use it as best we can. Can I suggest that some of the budget go to simple but impactful items such as cards for kids' birthdays (cheap cards are often available at the discount store). This has a huge effect on childrens' hearts, especially if you send it by post. We have had so many parents tell us how thrilled their children were that we knew it was their birthday and that we sent them a card. Likewise, your team members are precious and well worth celebrating. Send them a card or if they are one of your main room leaders then perhaps a little gift. This once again reaffirms that you value them. We had one year where a team member shared how much our card had meant to them as it was the only birthday card they'd received. The small things can have a really big impact.

Think strategically, don't just get a budget at the beginning of the year and spend it all by March! Plan it out, think about each month and what your requirements are. For example, how much does a Christmas bookmark or poster cost for each child? Do you need to put money aside to provide decorations or outfits for a Christmas performance in adult church. There are definitely times to restock the craft supplier, but make sure you don't get carried away.

It is helpful to spread finances across five key areas:

- Pastoral care (gifts and cards)
- Infrastructure (new technology, sport and play apparatus, and room furnishings)
- Consumable resources (craft & sensory items, labels for the printer system, allergy wristbands)
- Food (morning tea doesn't appear by magic)
- Reusable resources (things like board & card games, sensory craft elements you can reuse, dress-up costumes and toys)

Where will you store it?

Storage will depend upon your facilities, such as whether you have a cupboard or storeroom. Even if you have the budget to buy big infrastructure elements, it is no help if there's nowhere to put them. Expect to have some tricky conversations if you buy a huge ping pong table but haven't discussed with leadership beforehand about where it'll be stored. Sure, table tennis may be a God-inspired dream but be practical in your approach and talk these things through first.

Always try to streamline practicalities. For instance, if you have a large craft box that must be transported to kids church each week, consider transferring the contents into three smaller boxes. Thinking about these details will help you and your team stay sweet in your work (and it will protect your backs from lifting too much!).

One other thing to take into account is whether you can share resources. Perhaps another group in your church already has some of the infrastructure or non-consumable resources you require. For example, do the youth team have a bowling set? Could kids church use it on alternate weeks? We are one body and when it comes to resources we should work together and share resources where possible. That also includes a mutual understanding to look after all shared resources and return them to an agreed place.

Remember the more you are resourced, whether that's financially, with team members or with training, the more you can achieve – as long as you manage the resources well. Being a wise steward of your precious resources will enable you to do more for God in kids church. That said, faith dreams will always keep you on your knees for more resource! God never gives us faith dreams that only use up the resources we have. There will always be a stretch. If there isn't a stretch, then perhaps the dream isn't a faith one!

THE PRACTICALITIES

HE WILL BUILD HIS CHURCH

Rest well faithful one. It doesn't all lie on your shoulders. It's His house. If Jesus told us that He will build His church, and the gates of hell will not prevail against it, then any lack on your part is certainly not going to faze Him or even surprise Him! Remember He counted each hair on your head today too, not just the hair on the kids' heads that you love on each week!

When you've done all that you can to make kids church a safe and amazing place in which kids can encounter God - be at peace.

We are only called to offer God what we have, not what we don't have. At times, that might look like five very squashed loaves, and two smelly fish, but remember how much that makes the Father smile. He is more than able to do so very much more with our offering. What a joyous revelation - He wants to do more!

This is not a job that will ever get completed. In God there will always be far more to do, more ideas to have, a bigger team to care for - it will never be done. Be at peace in that place. Make sure that you schedule restful holiday times, and don't feel guilty for not being there while you're on holiday. Enjoy the time to rest, let it be a time of creativity and for God to speak to your heart and head! Heavenly strategy is ALWAYS the best strategy. If we're so busy in the doing, we will not hear those heavenly keys and we are more likely to struggle. Remember that Jesus said that He is the One who holds the keys to all realms (Rev 1:18). If there are problems in your team or kids that are on your heart, remember He has the key. Often we forget to ask Him for it.

Kids church is truly one of the highest callings. I do not believe that kids church is a stepping stone; a path to a greater role within adult ministry. As I've already mentioned, my husband and I have been a part of kids church for over 50 years between us. Nevertheless, we do have seasons in our lives. If you find yourself getting continually cranky or you feel like kids church has become a drudge of a duty rather than a joy, then have conversations with your leadership and share your heart. I don't mean when you are just having a rough day because nothing went to plan, that's just a bad day. I mean when you have been struggling for a prolonged period of time. It is vital that if you are not in a good place you have conversations around stepping out of functional roles before it causes you to end up in a bad heart place. The applies especially to a role with such a high level of function like kids church. No functional role or title is ever worth your place in God's house. Your church is your home. This is the family and body God has placed you in, and He has not limited you to a specific function forever. It can be hard to admit, but sometimes when you step back, it can be a way of guarding your heart. Stay sweet, choose to love His house and the Holy Spirit will come upon that choice and enable you.

Finally

God has placed you in His church to be, not just to do. So may His peace and joy strengthen you as you walk the wonderful adventure that is preparing a place for kids to encounter Him. May He multiply the impact of the work of your hands, and may you enjoy the crazy ride of faith that He has put you on! Hold on tight to Him!!! He is faithful.

ABOUT THE AUTHOR:

ANNE SILLARS

Anne Sillars and her husband, Paul, have been involved in a mixture of mission-based kids ministry and kids church for over 30 years. With a heart that champions our children's place within the local church, and decades of practical hands-on experience in both large and small churches, Anne's down to earth vision-filled approach will leave you excited to see God do more. Anne and Paul have been married for 30 years and they live in Brisbane, Australia with their two children.

* 9 7 8 1 7 6 4 2 8 1 3 2 4 *